KOALA

KOALA

WITH AN INTRODUCTION
BY THE AUSTRALIAN KOALA FOUNDATION

Thames & Hudson

NO TREE NO ME

DEBORAH TABART OAM
Chief Executive Officer
The Australian Koala Foundation

Nathan Ferlazzo
(Australia)
Buddha of the Bush
2015
Pen and ink

PREVIOUS PAGE
For Me By Dee/
Daniella Leo (Australia)
Kev the Koala
2015
Watercolour

When I was asked to join the Australian Koala Foundation (AKF) in 1998, my goal was to raise $5 million to go towards research at universities. At the time veterinarians were very worried about how the disease chlamydia was affecting koalas. When I joined the Foundation there were eighty-nine members and $17,000 in the bank. It soon became clear that raising money for such a beautiful creature was easy, but saving the koala was going to be a lot harder than anyone thought.

Within a year, funds were flowing in. We were also receiving phone calls from members of the public asking us to help stop development. I quickly realised, loss of habitat was a much more imminent threat to the koala than originally thought. It was clear we had to reconsider how and what the AKF could do to help. Our Chairman at the time was a strategic thinker and he said that we had to work out how to protect the trees – so our slogan 'No Tree No Me' was born.

We decided to work with a developer to see whether humans could live harmoniously with nature. I approached Brian Ray, a very successful developer, and although I must confess it did take some negotiation on both our parts, Koala Beach, a sustainable housing estate that broke conventional thinking was created. Koala Beach has now been running for twenty years; and koalas in Pottsville in northern New South Wales are relatively safe in a koala-friendly development.

At Koala Beach, humans fitted around the trees not the other way around. Trees were not cut down and our team of scientists worked with the project managers to ensure that the koalas living on the site, along with twenty-six other endangered species, were able to co-exist. It was a perfect model to counter the endless urban sprawl that has diminished so much of Australia's natural environment.

One of the greatest things about working on Koala Beach was meeting the local koala population. The whole site was 400 hectares and in the end 40 hectares was developed for humans and the koalas. The environment is now 360 hectares richer. This was my first encounter with capturing and radio tracking koalas. Our scientists started giving them numbers and I didn't realise it at the time, but all scientists around the world number their subjects so they don't form attachment to their subjects' personalities. However, I couldn't bear that. I frankly found it ridiculous and so I started giving the koalas names. There was Lulu, Marie, Arnie and 501, Arnie's father, who kept his number name. We tried to change it to Levi but it never stuck. We came to intimately know the lifestyles of fifteen koalas and it was completely fascinating.

We found that each male had his own territory. 501, the oldest koala, passed on his territory to his son, Arnie. Interestingly 501 seemed to roam the complete site at will, but the other males defended their territory at all costs. We learnt from both 501 and Arnie that there is hierarchy in a koala colony;

and best of all, we found out that the females' behaviour shaped the future and integrity of the gene pool. Marie, for instance, would pretend that she had a baby from two fellows – Arnie and Dennis – so that they would allow her and her joeys to roam freely across the whole landscape. Smart, eh? I am not sure that Arnie, the current King Koala, would have liked to have known this information though.

When I saw artist Luka Va's *King Koala* painted on the Eureka Tower, this story came to mind. Urban encroachment has destroyed so much of the koala's habitat and as you look at the beautiful images in this book, I hope you will spare a thought for the plight of all animals affected by urbanisation worldwide. We humans can live in cities, but the animals need forests, or as we call it in this country, the bush.

Just like real koalas, what I love about looking at the different and marvellous paintings, drawings and designs in *Koala* is their diversity. Diversity is what makes the world safe. Ecosystems have to be diverse to allow both the animal and human kingdoms to continue to enjoy fresh air, fresh water and fresh food. Here in Australia, we are also privy to a huge variety of birds and animal species that are unique to this wonderful and fragile place.

It is now nearly thirty years since I started and I've become know as the 'Koala Woman'. I love this title and I hear it everywhere I go. People look at me and say with interest, and sometimes bemusement, 'You're that Koala Woman, aren't you?'

There are many koala men and women who work tirelessly to help save the koala and the Australian bush but sadly it is a never-ending battle to save the trees. Everyone loves koalas, but it is too easy to get permission to cut down their habitats.

I am privileged to work for the Australian Koala Foundation and feel my team and I make a difference every day we go to work.

However, it is hard work and although I will continue to speak for the environment as long as I have breath, I need help and the koala needs you, the reader, to really make a difference. Humans must understand that we cannot have it all. We have to leave wild and beautiful places on 'this little blue globe' – as President Obama called it when speaking with Mr David Attenborough in 2016.

It is a small blue globe and each and every one of us can make a difference to keep it safe. Recycle, don't waste food, and take a water bottle out with you instead of buying a fresh bottle every time. Think about how you can make a difference, make one small change in your life that will either help a creature or the environment in some way. I sometimes think that we, in this modern and urban world, have forgotten how to be self-reliant, to think for ourselves. We can too often be looking to governments to solve our problems. However, the world is too complex for that now and we have to be resilient to face the changes that climate change brings to our lives.

The koala needs all of us to speak for them. Their job is to sit in the bush and give us immense pleasure, as I am sure this little book will give you.

Amber Gillett (Australia)
Helping Hand
2016
Charcoal pencil

Amber Gillett

Sammie Clark (USA)
Koala in the Treetop
2016
Ink, watercolour and waterproof pen

Koalas live in the tall eucalypt
forests and low eucalypt woodlands
of mainland eastern Australia,
and on some islands off the
southern and eastern coasts.

Queensland, New South Wales, Victoria and
South Australia are the only states where
koalas are found naturally in the wild.

Urška Kuplenik (Slovenia)
Mama Koala
2016
Digital

Australia has one of the highest

land clearing rates in the world

and it is estimated that 80 per cent

of koala habitat has already disappeared.

Christy Obalek (Canada)
Lazy Days
2016
Watercolour

Nicky Quartermaine Scott (USA)
Boomer
2015
Graphite

Sandra Phryce-Jones (Australia)
Koala
2012
Acrylic

Koalas in southern parts of Australia
are considerably larger and have thicker fur
than those in the north. This is thought to be
an adaptation to keep them warm in the
colder southern winters.

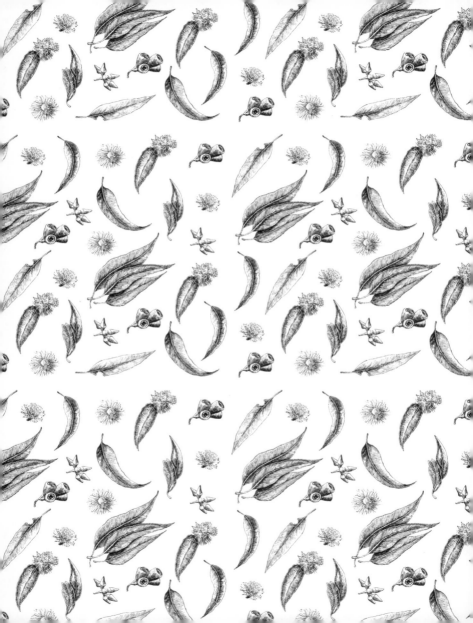

Koalas don't usually drink water unless in times of drought when leaves may not contain sufficient moisture.

Pete Cromer (Australia)
Koalala
2015
Paper collage

Different species of eucalypts grow in different parts of Australia, so a koala in Victoria will have a very different diet from one in Queensland.

Cohab Designs/Emily Tyers (Australia)
Bush Babe – Australian Koala
2016
Pencil, finished digitally

An adult koala eats between half a kilogram

to one kilogram of leaves each night.

Wiebke Rauers (Germany)
Koala with Ice Cream
2015
Digital

Koalas are very fussy eaters and have strong
preferences for different types of gum leaves.
There are over 600 varieties of eucalypts
in Australia.

Wiebke Rauers (Germany)
Sitting Koala
2014
Digital

Emma Morgan (Australia)
Golden Slumbers
2016
Pen, watercolour and gold leaf

ATTY/Graham Atwell (Australia)
Harold Koala
2016
Digital

Alex Doty (USA)
Koala Mama
2016
Ink

Koalas live in complex social groups

and contrary to popular opinion,

they are not migratory animals.

Each koala's 'home' is made up of several trees

called 'home trees' that they visit regularly.

Nidia Moreno (Mexico)
Where's my eucalyptus?
2016
Watercolour

I Ended up Here/Dan Adams (Australia)
Koala
2016
Digital

<u>RIGHT</u>
Loni Hsieh (USA)
Koala
2011
Digital

Baby koalas are called joeys.

John Butler (UK)
Koala Joey (from the book,
Whose Baby Am I?)
2001
Acrylic and pencil

D. Cerne

Before it can tolerate gum leaves,
which are toxic to most mammals, the joey must
feed on 'pap' – a specialised soft and runny
form of the mother's droppings.

Debbie Cerone (USA)
Koala Love
2015
Watercolour

Nathan Ferlazzo (Australia)
Koala & Joey
2014
Pen and ink

The joey stays in its mother's pouch for
about six or seven months, drinking only milk.

Brett Blumenthal (USA)
Mom and Baby Koala
2015
Watercolour and marker

Younger breeding females usually give birth

to one joey each year.

Afsaneh Tajvidi (Canada)
Koala and Baby
2013
Watercolour

When a joey is born, it's only about 2cm long.

It is also blind, furless and its ears

are not yet developed.

Brigitte May (Australia)
Far, Far Away
2015
Watercolour

TO:
FAR, FAR AWAY...

The joey leaves its mother's home range
between one and three years old, depending on
when the mother has her next joey.

Jay Fleck (USA)
Red Balloon
2014
Digital

Koalas are protected by law under
the Koala Protection Act. However around
80 per cent of their habitat is on
privately-owned land, most of which
is not protected by legislation.

Tiny Kiwi/Yolanda Kloppenburg (New Zealand/Germany)
Koala
2014
Digital

<u>RIGHT</u>
Studio Cockatoo/Kate Bordessa (Australia)
Koala
2015
Digital

Winter Avenue Press/Sally Gross (Australia)
Fly Koala Fly
2016
Pencil and watercolour

RIGHT
Sarah Jane Lightfoot (Australia)
Koala Hug
2015
Gouache and graphite

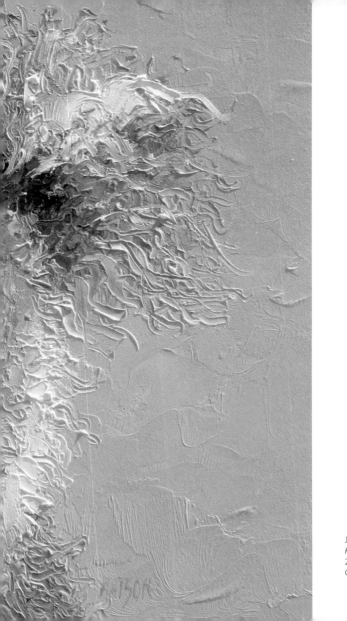

Jan Matson (Australia)
Koala
2015
Oil paint

Mulga (Australia)
Captain Kieran Koala
2014
Acrylic

The name 'koala' is thought to have meant
'no drink' in one of the Indigenous
Australian languages.

There is only one species of koala.
However, there are differing opinions amongst
the scientific community about whether there
are two or three sub-species of koalas;
or if there are any sub-species at all.

Depeapa/Verónica de Arriba (Spain)
Koala
2011
Pencil and digital colour

Animal Crew/T. McConnachie (Australia)
Koala Firefighter
2016
Graphite, paint and digital

Amber Lundy Leigh (USA)
Koala King
2012
Pen and marker

Jaqueline Burgess (Australia)
Koala Blue
2015
Watercolour and ink

Koalas are not bears but marsupials.

Fossil remains of koala-like animals have been
found dating back to 25 million years ago.

Kirsty Davidson (Australia)
Koala
2014
Gouache, acrylic and pencil

Leandra Vassolo (Argentina)
Koala
2012
Marker

The average life span of a koala
is about 10 years.

Catita Illustrations (Spain)
Koala
2014
Digital

Female koalas are fully mature by about

two years old. Males take a bit longer and

reach maturity by their third or fourth year.

L. Barrett
2011

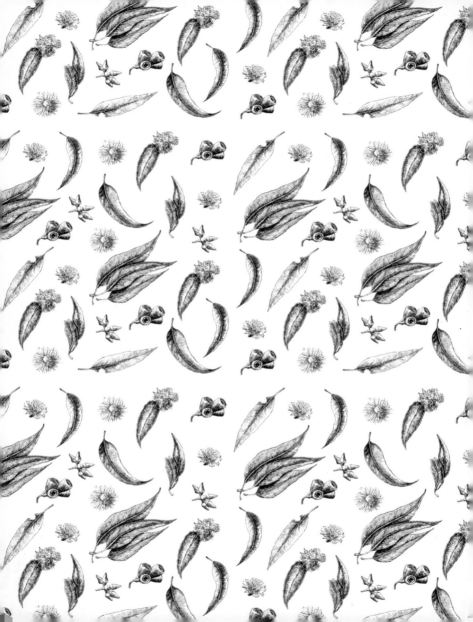

Contrary to popular belief,
koalas do not sleep twenty-two hours a day
because they 'get drunk' on gum leaves.
It actually takes a long time to digest
the leaves and sleeping is the most
efficient way to conserve energy.

PREVIOUS PAGE
Lesley Barrett (Australia)
Sleeping Koala
2011
Scratchboard

Kylie May Wilson (Australia)
Sleepy Koala
2016
Pencil

Koalas are mostly nocturnal.

Renée Treml (Australia)
Tea Cozy Koala
2013
Ink

Silke Powers (USA)
Just Hanging Out
2016
Acrylic

NEXT PAGE
Maria Taylor (UK)
Koalas in Pyjamas
2016
Watercolour, pencil and digital

Koalas have five digits on each front paw,

two of which are opposed to the others

much like our thumbs.

Wee Society (USA)
Kate the Koala
2012
Digital

Cat Rabbit (Australia)
Safety Blanket
2016
Gocco print

Ana Sanfelippo (Argentina)
Sumi (commissioned by the Stamp Study/
La Maraña Estampas, Buenos Aires)
2014
Ink and digital colour

Ashley Percival (UK)
Koala Skater
2015
Pencil, pen, paint and digital

<u>LEFT</u>
Ashley Percival (UK)
Koala Surfer
2015
Pencil, pen, paint and digital

Olivia York (Australia)
Suburban Gumtree
2016
Watercolour

Luka Va (Australia/Lithuania)
King Koala (on Eureka Tower)
2014
Ink pen and digital

Andreas Preis (Germany)
Koala
2012
Pencil, fineliner and marker

Habitat loss is the greatest threat to koalas.
The main reasons for this are land clearing,
bushfires and diseases of the eucalypt like
'dieback', which causes the trees to die.

A mature male koala has a scent gland

in the center of his chest that exudes a dark,

sticky substance. He rubs this on trees

to mark his territory.

One of the many ways koalas communicate

is by making a sound like a loud snore

and then a belch, known as a 'bellow'.

Merry Sparks (Australia)
How Much Can A Koala? No. 5
2014
Acrylic and glitter

Kerry Sparks

The Australian Koala Foundation estimates

that around 4000 koalas are killed by dogs

and cars alone each year.

Olga Inoue (Russia)
Koala
2016
Watercolour

Ellen Brenneman (USA)
The Spirit of Koala
2015
Acrylic and ink

Juan José Espinoza (Mexico)
Happiness of the Forest
2016
Watercolour and pastels

NEXT PAGE
Indi Dennis (Australia)
Rescue-Rehabilitation-Release
2015
Fineliner

ARTISTS

Afsaneh Tajvidi
joojoo.me

Alex Doty
adoty.com

Amber Gillett
ambergillettart.com.au

Amber Lundy Leigh
amberlundyleigh.com

Amy Borrell
amyborrell.com

Ana Sanfelippo
anasanfelippo.com.ar

Andreas Preis
designerpreis.com

Animal Crew/T. McConnachie
animalcrewshop.com

Ashley Percival
ashleypercival.com

ATTY/Graham Atwell
atty.com.au

Brett Blumenthal
tinytoesdesign.com

Brigitte May
brigettemay.com

Cat Rabbit
catrabbit.com.au

Catita Illustrations
catitaillustrations.com

Christy Obalek
christyobalek.com

Cohab Designs/Emily Tyers
etsy.com/au/shop/cohabdesigns

Debbie Cerone
etsy.com/shop/NurseryRembrandts

Depeapa/Verónica de Arriba
depeapa.com

Ellen Brenneman
ellenbrennemanstudio.com

Emma Morgan
emmamorgan.com.au

For Me By Dee/Daniella Leo
formebydee.com

I Ended Up Here/Dan Adams
iendeduphere.com

Indi Dennis
fourthcrossingwildlife.com

Jan Matson
janmatson.com

Jaqueline Burgess
jaquelineburgessart.com

Jay Fleck
jayfleck.com

John Butler
johnbutlerart.com

Juan José Espinoza
juan-jose-espinoza.pixels.com

Kirsty Davidson
kirstydavidson.com.au

Kylie May Wilson
kyliemay.com.au

Leandra Vassolo
leandrava.com

Lesley Barrett Scratchboard Art
lesleybarrett.weebly.com

Littlecatdraw
littlecatdraw.etsy.com

Loni Hsieh
TwoFishProject.com

Luka Va
luk.lt

Maria Taylor
mariataylorillustration.com

Merry Sparks
merrysparks.com

Mulga
mulgatheartist.com.au

My White Room/Olga Inoue
olgainoue.com

Nathan Ferlazzo
mariniferlazzo.com.au

Nicky Quartermaine Scott
studioQgallery.etsy.com

Nidia Moreno
Instagram.com/koalacita

Olivia York
oliviayorkdesign.com

Pamela Harnois
pamelaharnois.com

Pete Cromer
petecromer.com

Renée Treml
ReneeTreml.com

Sammie Clark
sjclarkart.com

Sandra Phyrce-Jones
Fineartamerica.com
colourinyourlife.com.au/
members/sandrapj

Sarah Jane Lightfoot
sarahjanelightfoot.com

Serena Chini
etsy.com/shop/Mydrops

Silke Powers
silkepowersart.com

Studio Cockatoo/Kate Bordessa
studiocockatoo.com.au

Tiny Kiwi/Yolanda Kloppenburg
tinykiwi.co.nz

Urška Kuplenik

Wee Society
weesociety.com

Wiebke Rauers
wiebkerauers.tumblr.com

Winter Avenue Press/Sally Gross
winteravenuepress.com.au

The Australian Koala Foundation (AKF) is a non-profit organisation dedicated to the conservation and effective management of the wild koala and its habitat.

Koala numbers continue to decline across Australia and the AKF is now 100% focused on enacting a Koala Protection Act: the purpose of which is to protect the koala's habitat, the lifeblood of the koala. Without their trees, koalas fall victim to dog attacks, car mortality, and worse still, starving to death.

The AKF believes there are no more than 100,000 koalas in Australia. Although there are no accurate numbers of koalas at white settlement in 1788, it is known that approximately 8 million skins were sent to market for fur from 1890 until 1927 and sold on both the London and New York fur trading stock markets. The AKF believes that it is possible to recover koala numbers, but the key is to protect the trees.

Serena Chini (Spain)
Mom and Baby Koala
2016
Watercolour and ink

'No Tree No Me.'
To learn more, visit: www.savethekoala.com

First published in Australia in 2016
by Thames & Hudson Australia Pty Ltd
11 Central Boulevard Portside Business Park
Port Melbourne Victoria 3207
ABN: 72 004 751 964

www.thameshudson.com.au

19 18 17 16   5 4 3 2 1

ISBN: 9780500500842

National Library of Australia
Cataloguing-in-Publication entry

    Koala
    9780500500842 (paperback)
    Koala–Australia–Pictorial works.
    Koala–Habitat–Conservation–Australia.
    Australian Koala Foundation.

599.250994

Front cover: Nathan Ferlazzo, *Koala*, 2015,
pen and ink on cotton rag
Back cover: Nathan Ferlazzo, *Koala & Joey*, 2014,
pen and ink on cotton rag
Inside cover: Nathan Ferlazzo, 2016
pen and ink

Design: Evi O
Printed and bound in China by 1010